the world

breaks

everyone

life, death and poetry

by S. N. Hayes

First Printing 2021
Paperback ISBN: 978-1-990467-34-9
Ebook ISBN: 978-1-990467-35-6

Cover, Book Layout and Print design
by East Coast Designs.
www.eastcoastdesigns.ca

Edited by Macie Gardner
The Editor with the Potter Tattoo
www.editorwithpottertattoo.com

imperceptions

Imperceptions Press
Oromocto, New Brunswick
www.imperceptions.com

dedicated to all those who have
felt lost, depressed, lonely, and broken.
there is life after pain.

"The world breaks everyone and afterward many are strong at the broken places. But those that will not break it kills. It kills the very good and the very gentle and the very brave impartially. If you are none of these you can be sure it will kill you too but there will be no special hurry."

— Ernest Hemingway, *A Farewell to Arms*

Author's Note

I am perhaps the last person I ever imagined would publish a book of poems. Not because I don't write poetry, but because I have always felt shackled by the *ideals* that others have of poetry. In grade school and then university, I was at odds with teachers who would tell me that my poetry wasn't following the rules. What rules? I struggled to mark my words as haiku or write stanzas that had the perfect amount of alliteration.

One of my strangest experiences with poetry came in a university class where the professor insisted for poetry to be *meaningful,* that it had to play with grammar, or in some ways, show a story through the physical words. I didn't agree. I tried to bend to these rules, but it didn't match my style.

When I wrote poetry, the technical matter of words was merely a tool, like a paint brush whisking away across the paper. To me, there are no rules in poetry—only emotions. Poetry can be overly dramatic, sappy, and often pretentious. Yet, every now and then, there is a truth to it that sweeps across the ages of time. I make no promises that my poetry will prevail. All I promise is that it is true, at least, to me.

Contents

"September 11th"

September 11th, 2000 was a regular day,
But no one was to know that one year later,
A bad attack would hurt the states.
The twin towers no longer stand.
Now it is 2003, 2nd anniversary.
Cry we must, pray we did.
Sad families ruined forever,
Never to see loved ones again
A war is stated down in Iraq
The States have suffered enough
Help they need.
But they'll stand till the very end.

Note: I wrote this poem when I was 10 years old (2003). It is my earliest surviving work. I make no claim that it's genius or profound, but it is part of my history and the evolution of my psyche.

"The Year I Never Saw"

One hundred years
Since the year I never saw
One hundred years watching,
Waiting
Wondering in awe.
I looked at you all,
As you grew, as you died too.
Like weeds you continued,
Flowering and disintegrating
As summers faded into cold fall.

So much has changed—
And yet, the world
Is still the same.
So much I have never done,
And never will.

We move through time
And yet, we change nothing.
A short life or a long life—
The end is the same.
Carved stone and 6 feet of sediment,
That hold your bones as flesh turns back
To feed the earth.

One hundred years
Since the year I never saw,
And yet, I still feel it—
I feel it all.

"Once"

I loved you once,
even though it was strange
I loved you through it all,
the inconvenience,
and the pain.
I loved you once,
then again.
I loved you twice-
and then a third.
I loved you,
even when it hurt.

"Walls"

The taller and stronger you build up those walls
in your mind,
the harder and slower they fall.
Sure, today you feel safe and secure, inside your
castle.
Tomorrow though, when the gates are
flooded—
and they come crashing in—
who will be your saviour?
You keep what loves you away
you press against all hope, so then,
when your demons come,
you are alone.

"Please"

I aim to please.
Please myself.
Excuse you.
Walk out of my way.
You're nothing.
I am everything.
No -
I will not listen.
I tried it your way,
weak, broken, shattered.
You are nothing.
I will walk away.
Before I am battered.
What will hold me back?
You've evaporated.
This glass
no longer has a crack.
I fixed me,
I deleted you.

"Faltered Reality"

Shot -
of *whiskey*
Shot -
of rum
Drown your sorrow in
a couple of coolers.
Shot -
of something that burns going down.
Shot -
Was that *vodka?*
Suddenly we're
on the dance floor
moving to songs I've never heard
skin *touches* skin
slowly,
then faster and longer
moving to a beat,
generating heat
Shot -
was that *tequila?*
Ten more minutes
two more,
move back to the floor
swaying to a new song.
The scene changes,
I can't remember how.

We're behind the wheel,
racing like the wind.
I feel your lips,
almost *numb*,
but they're there.
Kiss -
one two three
Kiss -
I can't remember my name
World's out of *control*,
It's all a blur.
Kiss -
I can't remember your name.
You touch,
I touch.
Blackout.

"Seven Sins"

I am proud of who I am,
I have passion that lusts for another,
I have wrath against those who
have wronged my loved ones,
I envy those who are at peace,
I am greedy when it comes to happiness,
I am sloth on my weakest days,
empty and amiss,
and sometimes I feel gluttony,
and consume too much
of this finite world.

"Closing Mind"

I am *lost*
and broken
I am the glass
that *shatters*
at your touch
not enough
is
too much
sinking
ending
suffocating

"Fast cars and girls who can't say no"

Damp eyes,
Open hearts,
Fast cars and
girls who can't
say no.
Spinning into the darkness,
clutch and shift
screeching tires
and metal scraping
we're flying towards
the light
in the endless night
how come everything so wrong
is so perfect,
so completely right
he moves his head to mine,
a kiss -
one more this time
his hands are on the wheel,
his eyes are on me.
I don't scream,
I let him kiss me
We risk it all -
for what?
He turns back to the road

the car lurches at his grip
I feel a surge of electricity
The heat between us dissipates,
But our hearts beat louder,
Threatening to pop out on the seat's leather.

"Trusting Love"

Transfixed by your heartbeat
I keep my hand on your chest
you breathe heavily
but it keeps me calm
we are waiting
waiting for the sun
but nothing but darkness
will come
how do I trust you?
When I know we are trapped.
I trust your voice
I trust your tapping fingers
and I trust your perfect chin
Even if we die tomorrow
I will have have known
the love and the feeling
of a love that's overgrown
it tangles like the weeds,
intertwining in your soul.
I will die not a half,
but a whole.

"Suicide Letter"

Wide eyed,
and short of breath,
my darling daughter
full of distress,
she looks to me
for all the answers
How though?
How could I offer
a shred of hope -
When all I see,
all I know,
is pain.
A mother's love
So strong -
so endless.
This could not stop
What my mind has held.
So I am sorry my dear,
For all your hurt
that I have caused.
So take with you,
in your heart,
that I have loved you
with every breath.

"To feel again"

I cut deeper now than I did before,
small soft lines,
have grown more jagged
I used to care
about each wound,
I'd clean them
as though it mattered
Now though the cuts
are full of pain
the pleasure long since waned,
but I feel something I thought
that I never could
again,
I feel alive each time I
slide the blade across my flesh
My legs and arms are littered
I'm damaged now you see,
So why would I stop this?
This horror I could be.
I think not of the future,
I think not of the past -
My life now revolves around
each drop of blood on glass.

"The Saddest Prose"

I never know what words I'll write,
when I start a piece of paper,
I never know the things I'll say,
when I type across my screen.
Yesterday I cared for the world,
today I'm selfish and sad.
Why just last week I wrote
the saddest prose,
but no emotions did I feel.
To look at every stanza
you might have thought I cared
but honestly,
I just can't change my mind.
Other's write when a feeling hits,
you know that deep gut-wrenching
thing they feel inside?
I write the saddest stories,
but only apathy do I feel
They say to stop -
to look and think
as though that's the way to change
but each time I say something
I can't help but not care.
You want another "great one"
you say this to my ear.
Well darling did the great's

have to live in such a world?
Plague cannot compare
to what I see today
more selfish and more rampant
than any tyranny.
I wonder if Sir Edgar,
had feelings just the same
remember when he asks
if it's all just a dream
within one never-ending dream?
I can't help but side with him
as I feel nothing for this world
perhaps though tomorrow I'll feel
but today,
It's all a hallucination -
brought on by a world of doubt

"In Death's Eyes"

Silence fills the spaces around the untouched
surface,
The sounds still rage, within my soul.
For you were with me then,
And you are with me now.
Alone I sit, filled with you.
Your essence more powerful than my breath,
The simple act of death,
You were there, or are you then?
Quietly searching my mind,
I find your picture, upon my breast.
Water seeping through the ceiling,
Dropping, and pattering.
Like the tears rolling down my cheek.
Noise begins to rise,
My own heart-beat taking me by surprise,
Is it really true?
Are we all equal in deaths eyes?
No one free,
We're all waiting for our demise.

"Witches in Dark Houses"

Witches in dark houses,
should not throw stones,
The earth shivers
and it breaks.
Whenever you **reject** nature
In such a way,
You will be torn
Inside and out
If you let the darkness
Overcome the light.
Where is the **broken** glass?
Is it on the floor?
Shattered into pieces
Dripping **blood**
And flesh and
Rotting plant
Ashes we have become
Miserable in our grave,
To live for all eternity
Death is frivolous
But I pray for it
Every second
Of every month

"Dead Silence"

I feel you at my side,
but how?
How could I feel you,
when you have all but
abandoned me,
years and years ago,
before they even knew
you, it was all you
why did it end this way?
The two of us together,
Intertwined

Why are you here with me?
Your grave has all but faded
but I am the one who has died
been dead since your last touch
but still, in my ear
nothing but your whispered voice
is all I hear

you drive me to the edge,
but never will I step
give myself to your ghost
for suicide will make me linger
these halls that held our love,
they also grip your soul
so if I wither on -

perhaps I will soar to heaven
away - to a better death
but first I must be here in hell
Your voice,
will be my fall.

"War"

You stepped out of line,
Through the cross-fire,
In the design of endless time,
One hundred summers could not ease the pain,
To which you inflicted upon a nation.
Suffering has become a new pain.
There are no children singing,
No larks above the war-torn soil.
The graves fill parks, and fields.
Death tearing through the cities like a knife
through silk.

"Stop!"

You press your hands to my back,
You grip my hand,
Won't let me go
Why do you torture me so?
I'm completely over you.
Yes it's true.
Get the fuck away from me.
I want to move on with my life.

Stop it,
Don't touch me.
Back to the first,
Here we are.
One more kiss.
Two more touches.
My body is relieved.
Of course I needed you.
Who else is there to need?
Oh god don't stop.
I want to kiss you back.
I have to kiss you back.
There is no one else.

My god.
Keep going.
Wait, where are you going?

Once more you leave me alone.
Of course, I was so naïve.
Go fuck yourself.
Wait?
I didn't mean it.
Come back!

"All the Words I Never Said"

They all say it's not my fault
But fault doesn't equate hurt
They say you made your own choices –
And you did
You chose, chose to go
But I didn't choose to stay

My hand could have held yours
My lips, cruel and twisted,
Could have been kind
I could have showed you

But you chose to go,
But I didn't choose to stay

Self pity, and every tear
Gulty-stained memories,
And it doesn't change a thing.
I hear your voice, but I don't hear it in my ear.

Your words are splintered across my soul
Of childhood days – and missing you
The lingering smell of the pillow when you'd
gone

I see your face stained red,

From metal I flayed
But you smiled
And you begged us to stay
But, we didn't choose to stay

How do I live with those words
The ones I left behind
When you chose to leave,
But I could have chosen to stay
To let the words fall on your ears,
When you could hear them and it would matter

You may be gone,
But I choose to stay—
To love you,
All you have left,
And all that you were.

"Blind Arrogance"

As you stare upon your leg,
Blood, mixed with anxiety and pain,
Clouds of hunger,
As you scratch towards the vein.
"A dangerous time to let your
Head make up its own mind."
Think of all the words you've heard.
Now hasn't this just become absurd?
Doubt is no where near.
There's nothing left to hear.
Another poem written,
Some one sheds a tear.
"You're deep."
They say and you smile.
Thinking of the wound upon your thigh,
Your misery hiding in plain sight

"Zeus' Kingdom"

Heaven's song and shallow eyes
As Poseidon takes a final bow.
Great new year,
After millennia, we toe –
Yet, still we breathe winter's glow.
As time passes and moves –
And the god's chariot flies –
We remain chained.
The clay of what we were born,
Still at our feet
And Prometheus, does he cry
Because of what we have done with the gift
Of fire?
Torn by ash, and men take metal for towers
And for chambers in their gun –
Yet we think we are not beneath them?

"Cold Tea"

I sit beside my world,
thinking of the end
there is nothing such as sweet
as cold tea on warm days
you walked away
I let you,
but forever will I sit
dreaming of that tea
and what it could have meant

"A life that could have been"

I never dreamt of love,
I never wanted to belong to another.
I want a life of solitude
Of short days
And long books,
Near fireplaces
Even clubs
Or drinks of whiskey
But not a life of you and I
My best friend has always been
The one I held so dear,
Though myself that may be
I never regretted a year.
Then I was hurt by another,
A friend I held to my heart
I swore then I would never
allow some one to be
Everything to me
You came to love me though,
You brought me out of shadows
And I saw the light in you
That I never saw in myself
I loved you every minute
Right until the end
I went back to my normalness
To being my only friend

But you know,
I still think sometimes
Of when you told me things
We dreamt of a life together
Of a sort of normalcy.
I wonder how you are today
Happy just to be
A part of you for one short time
Of what you meant to me
Not every story is forever,
But not every story is true
But darling I could never lie
Not when it's about you.
So go on now and live your life
Live it without me
But some nights when you're cold,
Think of all the memories we hold
Of a world that could have been

"The Great Scar"

How can I feel so paralyzed,
By what I don't achieve?
When all your days
Ended before my own age?
I feel so lost—I'm tired and yet
All I want to do is more.
I want the world to bend at my feet
And I want to learn everything
Read every book,
See every film, and hear
Every song that has ever played.
Am I selfish to feel such lack of
Pride in all I have done?
When your journey ended before
You got 25 years around this
Golden gleaming sun?
I'm struggling to decide
What's worth the time
If anything at all is—
Or if we're all just
Searching for the time to
Decide who we are
Before our days go out too,
Like candles that extinguish in a subtle
Gust of wind.
Is life nothing but a collection

Of flesh, bone, ash and scar?

"Alone"

There is darkness in my world,
it watches me as I sleep.
My heart is broken
into pieces,
shattered ones,
tiny little shards
of jagged glass.
I dare you to try
and fix me,
you'll be bloody
by the end.

"Man, the Political Animal"

Whether King and Castle
Or Minister and House
The longest chess game continues
And we are all just Shakespeare's
Fools, strutting along our stage.
March with words or swords,
Avenge, fight, beat and trample.
There is always another mantle.

"Stardust"

It's a beautiful ugly thing
A princess you must be,
Sparkling in the eternal sea.
Your hair glows brighter—
than any earthly sun.
Even with your demise
You seem to have won.
The night sky shines a little more
Each time your smile beams
And opens love's endless door
For all my loss,
I do not shed a tear,
For even when they disappear,
All that matters cannot be destroyed

"Growing up"

I cannot remember my childhood fears,
I suppose that is something,
I've lost over the years.
Love has gone over my head,
and I've never considered
that someday I would be dead.
I live for myself,
but I cry for those
who cannot have
the simple things.
I try to be nice,
but nothing can stop
the way that I feel
for a world that has lost
all that is good.

"Here I am Without You"

You opened my eyes,
I want them closed.
How could you have opened my heart?
I told you I'd never love again.
You swore to change my mind.
You bastard, you stole it all.
You stole my peace, my serenity.
I loved you more than I'd even loved before.
The pain was gone, and you were there.
Now you're gone, how could you?
Did you plan this all along?
No, you'd never want to die,
But you did, how could you?
Here I am, without you,
I hate this.

"Christmas Now"

Lights trickle as the spirits glow,
Screeching, wailing through my heartful
struggles.
As I try to bargain with my soul.
Of dinners past, and memories that once met
In chapels and singings choirs that brought
warm tears
That trickled as softly as the white pure and
sparkling snow.
My red lips, and cold hands,
As I look upon the mirror – I should see
happiness
– should feel warmth as I glimpse upon the tree.
Instead I worry and wonder.
I fear as the bitter poison spreads through
arteries and vein—
Pressure and misery bringing me
Under the surface of the depths of an ice-frozen
sea.

"At Shore"

Fog envelopes the town
Touching as far
as the windowpane
of a woman
So sad
as her eyes try to gaze
Past smoke
And unto the
Hidden shore
Thick mist
Grazes fingers that
Paw at the air
Desperately
How long He was gone Ticked off on the Sill,
Little marks, day by day, *Scraped* into the wood
"Come home,"
she whispers
to the fog
Water grazes her skin, Searing as it
f
a
l
l
s
Across her soft face Like the sea, salty, Touches
her lip
and makes a bitter kiss

"Frozen"

Her eyes are heavy,
blue and icy.
The shadows in her pupils
warn me,
tell me to leave.
If I could search them,
I might find the answer to many mysteries
in their depth.
I do not.
I only gaze at the
calm and glistening surface.
The sun reflects against those eyes,
at first glance,
they seem so innocent.

I fear that if I were to venture further
I may crash through thick, frozen layers.
If that were to happen,
I may spend my last moments with no breath.
I would be suffocated by the darkness.
Her eyes are greater
than any lake that I explored
as a child,
expansive, and endless.
I hear my mother hollering to me,
"Stay away from that lake,"

she'd say, voice stern.

Just as I had crept upon the frozen water,
I do not listen.
I stare into the eyes of the sea,
longer than I should.
If I were any other man,
I might be distracted by the fullness,
her naturally stained lips.
I cannot be bothered by these details.

Behind the thin strip of glass there are thoughts,
Thoughts the toughest man could not endure.
There are emotions that I terrorize,
In their calm silence, her eyes whisper,
"danger".

I know nothing of her suffering,
I want to hold her arms in mine,
tell her that there are days that warm.
There is sunshine and beaches
that stretch against the shores in the summer,
and there is swimming, and laughing.
I wish to tell her of a time of year when the
water,
when the expanse,
is to be enjoyed instead of endured.
I say nothing.

She watches me closely,
so loud in her silence.
I feel myself fall through her eyes,
nothing to hang on to –
the surface breaks away.

I am plunged beneath the waves.
The weight and heaviness of her thoughts,
push me down further,
I cannot escape.
If I could, I would not,
I am content to stay here.
I am trapped forever in her icy hands,
I am cold,
but I am loved.

"Ash"

My head spins
My breath shortened
The bright lights blind me
I take a step
My mind freezes
You drive forward
I cannot hide—
You step beside me
With subtle control
I mix in your crowd

Call my name
Without a sound
You move a hand
I come around
We start to fight—
I give in.
You knock me down.
I help you up.

"The Contentment of Loneliness"

Loneliness grapples me like an old friend,
Hand in hand as it embraces my middle,
As I fall asleep – tossing and turning,
It switches sides of the bed with me.
Loneliness is content to hold me as I sleep.
It never snores.

Nor does it ever complain that I like the room
cold,
Yet have thick blankets to compensate.
Loneliness is there with me as tears trickle down
my cheek
But it does not wipe them,
I have to do it myself –
And I do.

Loneliness is most content and active
As the flowering world outside darkens and dies
off
Into winter. It strives and flourishes as all else
dies,
Like the weeds which grow through February
snow.

It will sit as you read a book,

And it will tug at your chest and pull your
muscles
As you read about romance,
Tucked in your heat as wet snow wells on your
window,
And the branches of long-dead trees tap against
the glass,
Threatening to break inside.

Loneliness is content to follow as bitter winds
Slap your face and as the air becomes so thick
with cold
That your hands and face become burned by
frost.
If only loneliness were but a season.

"The Death of Thinking"

The greatest horror of the modern age
As it sweeps further and further
And cameras keep spanning past further
generations,
And men – oh how we see them,
On their screens – even videos,
Incriminating words they speak.
Oh, it's such a horror because now
We see – our idols, are not
Immortals.
They laughed, and joked,
And they even fell flat,
On their faces.
Their morals were not clandestine.
There will be no more Shakespeare's,
Or Hobbes',
There can be no new iteration
Of Kings and great wars.
Because even the wars
Play out on our screens.
Capturing images of the blows,
And we see the blood
And can almost taste the sulphur
And hot metal as new bombs fly.
There are no secrets anymore,
No whispering fractures that survive

Time, but leave us wanting more
Because – the generations after
They will have the more –
And they will not want to see.
For their own men will be trite and filmed,
And sharing so much that words
Will become nothing more than letters
Like Alphabet Soup.
Perhaps words, and paintings –
Will go out of favour.
Replaced by flashing images
From some new device.
Why must one think when it's all there,
Spelled out – the words spoken again
And again
And again
Until it all loses meaning.

"Modern Apathy"

Sometimes I gaze back on words I wrote,
tragedy after tragedy.
Words of hope and consolation.
Hope of change and for a world
Without pain.

I wonder now,
Where she is.
That girl that cared.
Who loved and held esteem
For favouring the strong
And hugging the burdened.
Has the world
In its darkness
Pushed her head under water?
Drowned whatever caring and love
That she once held.

Has she simply picked up the sword
For another cause –
Too busy advocating and changing
Another shore
To look at the faces of the dead
Or, has she simply come to face
That humanity will always exist

With a sense of dread?

I wonder if she is simply tired
Hibernating as this long winter
Looms over the earth.
Will she return?
In full strength –
Ready to fight, to care
To love.

"Greatest Fear"

I always wished I'd find
Somebody to hold my hand
To wipe away my tears
and help me feel grounded on dry land.
I thought you'd take away my fears.
But, now that I have loved you,
I have never felt so scared.
How could I go on if I lost us?

"City vs. Shore"

There's a war within me—
One that's existed for one hundred and ten
years
My grandmother, and her grandmother
Both fought the same drawn-out battle.

How can one simply choose the city or country?
A world of field or one of stone and metal?

Our families all seem to choose country
The sea and hearth so close you can
Taste the salt on your morning breath

I cannot choose between the two.
I wander back and forth, from the sea's shores
To the city and its large department stores.

When I was young, I dreamt of Manhattan—of
buildings that
Stood with the skies.
Now as I sit in my home,
By the city where I often roam
I dream of the shore,
Of the *"heather and the hills"*
And the simple pleasures that
Enticed my childhood imagination

And when I go back
And sit on the hill by the shore,
All I can think is—how much longer?
How much more?
Until I am back in my city,
Torn between two homes—
Never to be sure.

"Writer's Block"

I simply cannot write poetry
When I am in love –
I don't see the same colors,
Everything is tinted by the blue of your eyes.
I can't think of pain, or death, or
Even metaphors of wilting fall flowers –
All I see are your hands as they graze my knee.
I try to write, but all that comes out
Are playful words that I say to you.

Shaylynn Hayes is the author of *Full of Sound and Fury* and *Acceleration*. Her books can be found on Amazon. Shaylynn has a Bachelor of Arts in Political Science, and an Honours Diploma in Creative Digital Media. Shaylynn is a writer, graphic/web designer, political science enthusiast, and lover of flowers and the ocean. Shaylynn comes from Cape Breton Island, Nova Scotia, but has always been fascinated with fast-paced, morally ambiguous stories. Some of her favourite books include *Savages* by Don Winslow, *Beautiful Disaster* by Jamie McGuire, and classics like *Wuthering Heights*, and *Pride and Prejudice*. Shaylynn also likes to take influence from television and loves shows like *Gossip Girl, 90210, Pretty Little Liars, Desperate Housewives, Dead To Me*, and really anything where character-driven mistakes cause drama. And of course, Shaylynn loves car films, with particular love for *The Fast and the Furious, Smokey and the Bandit*, and *Need for Speed*.

Twitter: @Imperceptions
Facebook: www.facebook.com/ShaylynnHayes
Instagram: @imperceptions
Website and Blog: www.shaylynnhayes.com